More Codes for Kids

Weekly Reader Books presents

More Codes for Kids

BURTON ALBERT, JR.

Illustrated by
Jerry Warshaw

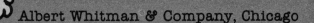

Albert Whitman & Company, Chicago

To
MOM . . .
and the memory of
. . . DAD

This book is a presentation of
Weekly Reader Books.

Weekly Reader Books offers book clubs for children
from preschool through junior high school.

For further information write to:
Weekly Reader Books
1250 Fairwood Ave.
Columbus, Ohio 43216

Library of Congress Cataloging in Publication Data

Albert, Burton
  More codes for kids.

  SUMMARY: More codes for cryptanalysts to crack, many
with jokes or riddles for answers. Includes among others,
a Code-a-Nut Tree and Backflip Triple Decker codes.
  1. Ciphers—Juvenile literature. [1. Ciphers]
I. Warshaw, Jerry. II. Title.
Z103.3.A535   001.54'36   79-245
ISBN 0-8075-5270-4

Cracking codes is like munching popcorn. After you sample some, you want more.

That's what happened when you first tasted **Codes for Kids**: you asked for **More Codes.** Now here you are, 25 new Master Code Keys and 124 Mystery Messages—437 secret words— for you to crack and check in the Answer File on page 30. It's a feast of fun!

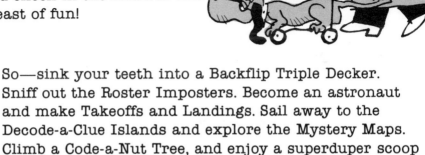

So—sink your teeth into a Backflip Triple Decker. Sniff out the Roster Imposters. Become an astronaut and make Takeoffs and Landings. Sail away to the Decode-a-Clue Islands and explore the Mystery Maps. Climb a Code-a-Nut Tree, and enjoy a superduper scoop of Butter-Riddle Ripple.

HOORAY!
RIDDLES & LAUGHS
Yes, there are rib-ticklers, too, with punch lines for you to decode and chuckle about.

Be careful. Don't leave any popcorn kernels along the way.
In other words, don't write or mark in this book. That would put spies on your trail. Keep the coded messages a secret from every kid who follows you, from the flip of this page on. Happy Code Crackin'!

CATER-RIDDLE-PILLAR

This little critter hides a coded letter in each part that stands alone. Together, the letters spell out the answer to a riddle. For example:

What isn't much good until it's dropped?

PL A NEA CH ST O RE R OOM = ANCHOR

Try the Key: Crack the Codes

Which fur is warmest?

1 F DND YO U RNA DL AT ON CE

What's made of three bees, a bull, and you?

2 B UIO URTO B B YA L E ADER

What can't be seen without a closed eye?

3 PL A YS WD TH N INE K IDS

What's the temperature in a beehive?

4 PU SH ME W DTH TH A TB R OOM

How well did you do? Inch along to the **Answer File** on page 30.

TOTEM POLES

To carve out the message hidden in a totem pole, read from top to bottom. Look for each word that has this kind of arrow ↑ **before** or **after** it.

Try the Key: Crack the Codes

1
→ MY
DEAR ↑
FRIEND ↓
↖ A
↑ CODE
PAL ↑
← HAS
READ ↑
EACH ↑
WORD ↙
THE →
↑ POLE
ON ↑
THIS ↑
CORNER ←
PAGE ↑

2
THEN ↑
↘ IF
YOU'LL ↑
↑ LEARN
TO ↙
→ DO
THAT ↑
MAYBE ↙
↑ I'D
↓ GO
LIKE ↑
THERE ↓
TO ↑
↑ START
→ NOW
↑ A
BUY ↙
→ ONE
↑ MAGAZINE

3
PLEASE ↙
↘ FORGET
↑ IT
WILL ↑
→ YOU
↑ BE
IT →
WRITTEN ↑
↖ DOWN
ONLY ↑
IN ↑
TRUTH →
↑ CODES
← ARE
THAT ↑
PAL ↑
↑ CLUBBERS
↙ SURE
KNOW ↑

4
THEY ←
WOULD ↑
← LIKE
YOU ↑
TO →
↑ LIKE
→ THEM
TO ↑
→ GO
↑ HELP
WITH ↑
↑ THE
FIRST ↑
→ TIME
↑ ISSUE
A →
NOTICE ↙

BALLOON BUFFOON

Have a circus of fun—send a message by balloon.

1 Write your message in the everyday way.

2 Break the message into strange-looking letter sets. The number of sets will tell you how many balloons to make.

3 Draw the balloons in an order which clearly shows how they are to be read, beginning at the top and going from left to right.

4 Fill in all the balloons with the same color. Write the letter sets on the balloons in the order that they should be read.

5 Then add balloons of another color or two and write different sets of letters on them. These are **misleads.** A mislead is any letter, word, or mark which hides a message.

6 Add strings and let the balloons go—to a friendly code-cracker who knows which color to read.

Try the Key: Crack the Codes

Color orange is the clue for you.

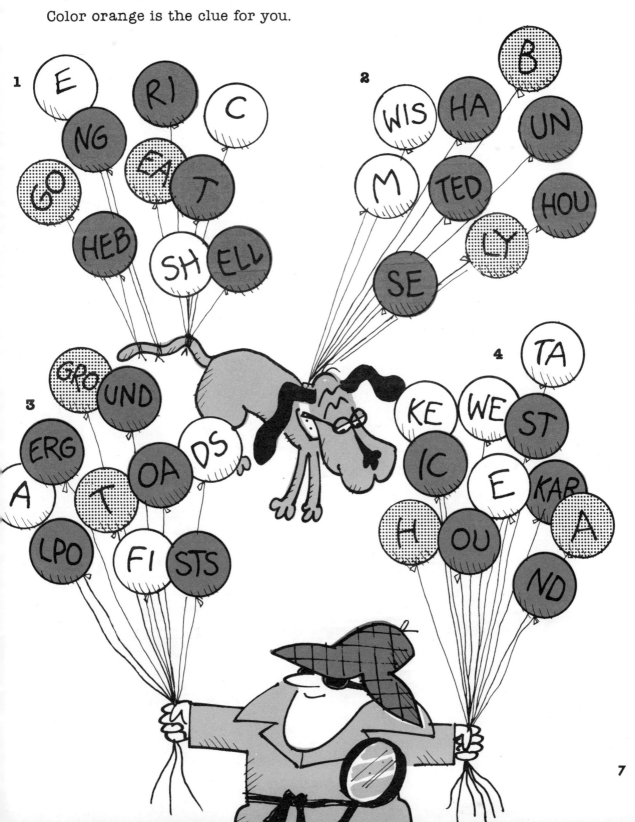

SHOE BUSINESS?

Spies will think you're a real heel when they see a
message written in something that looks
like shoe sizes:

9 1½   4 2½ 8½ 2 12 5   7½ 1 12 11

But those in the know can
figure it out easily with this key:

1	2	3	4	5	6	7	8	9	10	11	12	13	•	1½	2½	3½	4½	5½	6½	7½	8½	9½	10½	11½	12½	13
A	B	C	D	E	F	G	H	I	J	K	L	M	•	N	O	P	Q	R	S	T	U	V	W	X	Y	Z

Here's how it works. A numeral by itself (9, for example) signals
the position of a letter in the first part of the alphabet (I).
A numeral with a fraction (1¹/₂) signals the position of a letter
in the **last half** of the alphabet (N).

So, in the message above, 9 1¹/₂ means IN. The rest of the message
answers this riddle: How does a two-headed monster speak?

Try the Key: Crack the Codes

1	3½ 1 3 11 1 12 8½ 1½ 3 8
2	10½ 1 9 7½ 8½ 1½ 7½ 9 12 4 1 5½ 11
3	5½ 9 4 5 7½ 8 5 6 5 5½ 5½ 9 6½ 10½ 8 5 5 12
4	10½ 8 1 7½ 4 9 4 12½ 2½ 8½ 7 5 7½
5	9 7½ 6½ 6½ 2½ 6 8½ 1½ 1½ 12½.
6	10½ 8 12½ 6½ 8 2½ 8½ 12 4 9
7	9 8 1 9½ 5 3½ 9 5 5½ 3 5 4 5 1 5½ 6½
8	6½ 7½ 9 3 11 2 1 12 12 7 1 13 5 1 7½ 6½ 9 11½

GHOST HUNTERS, Inc.

3 12 8½ 2   13 5 7½   2½ 1½   13 2½ 1½ 4 1 12½.

13 5 5 7½ 9 1½ 7   6½ 7½ 1 5½ 7½ 5 4   12 1 7½ 5.

5 9½ 5 5½ 12½ 2½ 1½ 5   2 8½ 7½   5½ 2½ 12½

9½ 2½ 7½ 5 4   7½ 2½   7 2½   7 8 2½ 6½ 7½

8 8½ 1½ 7½ 9 1½ 7   1½ 5 11½ 7½   6 5½ 9 4 1 12½

1½ 9 7 8 7½.   13 5 5 7½ 9 1½ 7   5 1½ 4 5 4   17½

6 9 9½ 5.

8

BACKFLIP TRIPLE DECKERS

Feed a hungry code-breaker. Try this recipe for a triple-deck sandwich. Whip up a message:

COME TO THE CLUBHOUSE

Break the words into **triplets**—sets of three letters each:

  1 | 2 | 3 | 4 | 5 | 6

COM|E TO|THE|CLU|BHO|USE

Stack the triplets in this backflip pattern:

²ETO | ¹COM
⁴CLU | ³THE
⁶USE | ⁵BHO

And, if needed, add a dash or two of final misleads.

Try the Key: Crack the Codes

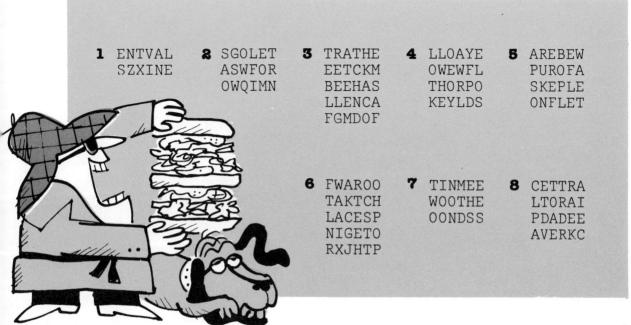

1 ENTVAL SZXINE	**2** SGOLET ASWFOR OWQIMN	**3** TRATHE EETCKM BEEHAS LLENCA FGMDOF	**4** LLOAYE OWEWFL THORPO KEYLDS	**5** AREBEW PUROFA SKEPLE ONFLET

6 FWAROO TAKTCH LACESP NIGETO RXJHTP	**7** TINMEE WOOTHE OONDSS	**8** CETTRA LTORAI PDADEE AVERKC

ROSTER IMPOSTERS

When you drop an **O** from **rooster**, you don't get a goose egg. Instead, you get a list of names called a **roster**. And you can use such a list to crow about something—in code.

First, print or write the letters of your message down a zigzag column. Then hide each letter in the message with a person's name that ends with the same letter.

STEP 1

S
K
A
T
E
B
O
A
R
D

STEP 2

GLADYS
JACK
SARA
DOT
DAVE
BOB
MARIO
LILA
ROGER
TED

Try the Key: Crack the Codes

1. PEG
CLEO

NINA
LEW
FIONA
GARY

2. Rich
anna
Bill
Sal
otto
Winslow
Lucille
Louise
Jan

3. Kip
Pu-Yi
Megan
Chic
Ruth

Tish
Billi
Walt

4. ROD
LOU
VIC
KIRK

JO
ESAU
GERT

5. alan
Lo

marcia
Fran
Doris
matthew
Eve
Adar

6. SIMON
LULU
HARRIET
LES

NAT
RODRIGO

KELLEY
HUGO
CHI-CHOU

7. RAJ
MYRA
MARC
NICK
SKIP
BOBO
MILT

8. Jeff
angelo
Heather
jack

fifi
Curt

Spiro
Bev
Steve
amber

INITIAL IT!

John S. Lomax
Phyllis U. Conte
N.S. Peck
Mary E. Czak
T. Harold Ryan

You can also tuck messages behind initials in a roster.

John **S.** Lomax	S
Phyllis **U.** Conte	U
N. S. Peck	NS
Mary **E.** Czak	E
T. Harold Ryan	T

} = SUNSET

Try the Key: Crack the Codes

1
Beth W. Masi
I. S. Rosebaum
E. G. Ward
Max U. Reiner
Lucy Y. O'Neill

2
H. E. Santo
Tina L. Mikos
P. M. Logan
Sam E. Lui

3
T. W. McAvoy
Jean O. Rasky
D. Carl Tice
I. M. Vernon
E. S. Selig

4
Carol D. Marsh
O. N. Evans
Gail T. Webster
Wah R. Cheng
Britt I. Larsen
S. K. Levin
Cary I. Archer
T. William Hayes

5
Cruz O. Correa
N. T. Meyer
Sue H. Robbins
E. D. Schmidt
James O. Fipps
C. K. Togo

6
B. R. Renzi
Floris I. Polk
N. G. Withers
Nancy B. Mendez
Gladys O. York
O. T. Wylie
Karen S. MacLean

7
F. A. Leung
C. Edward Gans
E. T. Laffont
Ann H. Nesbit
E. M. Perri
Olive U. Sayles
S. I. Chin
Earl C. Stoll

8
H. Peter Borrows
A. S. Thomas
Kay S. Hardy
Fred H. Dixon
Sylvia E. Boyd
G. O. Blaustein
Paul N. Cooper
Sally E. West

9
Betty C. Coscia
A. L. Goff
Nina L. Kurtz
Jack I. Malloy
T. Fiore
Sol O. Perlman
Judy F. Jones
F. Harris Halton

TAKEOFFS AND LANDINGS

Scan this airport television screen for departures. Notice the numerals in color. They come after a colon (:), and each provides a signal that leads to a letter in the name of the city on the same line.

For example, the 4 in 8:41 means count in to the fourth letter, the J in San Jose. The 1 in 9:10 means track down the E, the first letter in Elmira.

DEPARTURES

8:41	SAN JOSE
9:10	ELMIRA
11:08	WASHINGTON

DEPARTURES

8:41	SAN JOSE
9:10	ELMIRA
11:08	WASHINGTON

A zero (O), however, doesn't signal any letter in this code. It signals the numeral after the zero. In 11:08, the zero signals the 8, and that numeral leads to the T, or eighth letter, in Washington. Together, the numerals track the word JET.

Try the Key: Crack the Codes

1

9:15	DENVER
10:36	SEATTLE
11:55	FRESNO
1:38	MACON
2:50	BOISE

2

12:13	HARTFORD
1:56	CANTON
2:30	PITTSBURGH
3:11	DALLAS
4:27	HOUSTON
5:06	CHICAGO

3

4:36	MOBILE
5:09	KNOXVILLE
5:53	DUBUQUE
6:29	JUNEAU
8:40	SPRINGFIELD
9:49	TOPEKA
10:07	CHARLOTTE

4

11:08	RICHMOND
12:19	RACINE
1:02	TULSA
2:50	TACOMA
3:14	SPOKANE

5

8:45	TAMPA
9:48	SHREVEPORT
10:10	GRAND RAPIDS
11:36	DULUTH
12:04	SUPERIOR
1:45	FARGO

SUM-ER TIME

The numerals that stand for hours and minutes can also conceal messages. Add the numerals for each time and match the sum to its letter position in the—

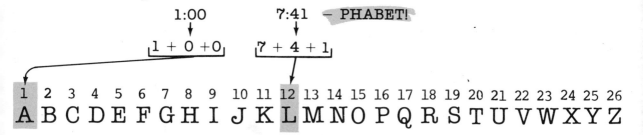

	1:00		7:41 – PHABET!
	↓		↓
	1 + 0 + 0		7 + 4 + 1

1	2	3	4	5	6	7	8	9	10	11	12	13	14	15	16	17	18	19	20	21	22	23	24	25	26
A	B	C	D	E	F	G	H	I	J	K	L	M	N	O	P	Q	R	S	T	U	V	W	X	Y	Z

But beware! Watch for the double digit numerals 10, 11, and 12 **before** the colon (:). Treat them this way,

Go— 12:45   11:05

12 + 4 + 5   11 + 0 + 5

↓   ↓

21   16

↓   ↓

U   P —AND AWAY!

Try the Key: Crack the Codes

1	2	3	4	5	6
2:01	4:04	1:05	10:19	11:44	5:14
1:00	9:24	4:14	1:00	7:49	10:29
5:27	11:02	12:48	8:30	1:00	9:05
1:03	5:00		2:03	8:41	4:12
11:59	12:29	2:00		7:18	3:45
	7:17	4:01	11:45	1:04	5:00
3:00	12:15	11:38	2:24	3:01	
1:00	6:50	9:19	3:02	5:00	12:07
8:51					1:00
2:30	10:29	3:43	11:33	1:00	4:11
	2:32	3:20	8:58	3:14	1:00
	1:07	3:11	5:04	1:13	10:35
		12:04	12:59	1:00	5:22
				4:00	

CODE-A-NUT TREE

On a code-a-nut tree, only a branch with a two-leaf tip bears a secret word. Climb up the left side of the tree, then down the right —

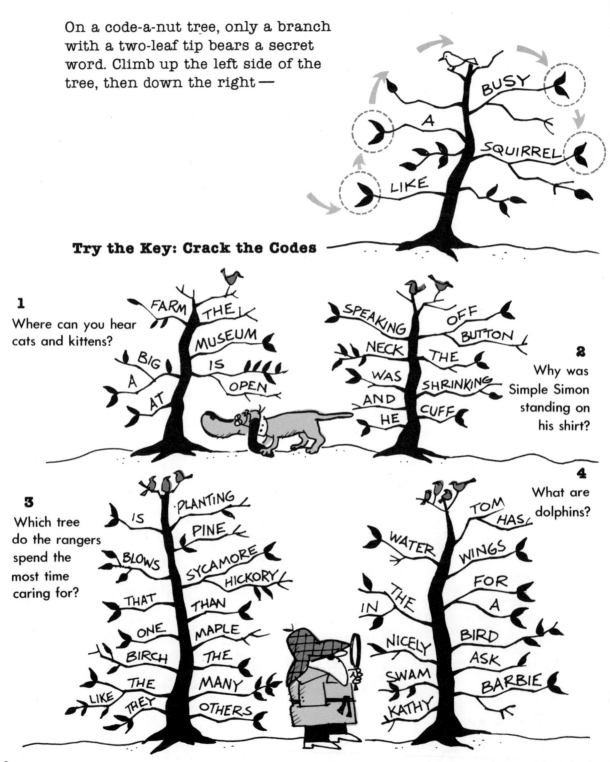

BUSY

A

SQUIRREL

LIKE

Try the Key: Crack the Codes

1

Where can you hear cats and kittens?

FARM

THE

MUSEUM

BIG

IS

A

OPEN

AT

2

Why was Simple Simon standing on his shirt?

SPEAKING

OFF

BUTTON

NECK

THE

WAS

SHRINKING

AND

HE

CUFF

3

Which tree do the rangers spend the most time caring for?

IS

PLANTING

PINE

BLOWS

SYCAMORE

HICKORY

THAT

THAN

ONE

MAPLE

BIRCH

THE

THE

MANY

LIKE

OTHERS

THEY

4

What are dolphins?

TOM

HAS

WATER

WINGS

THE

FOR

IN

A

NICELY

BIRD

ASK

SWAM

BARBIE

KATHY

14

JUMPIN' JU>PI<TER!

Although these messages may look like computer feedback from a space satellite, they're easy to decode. Just search for either of these two signs: > or <.

When you come to this >, look at the numeral which follows it. The mark and the numeral together tell you how many more jumps **ahead** you must make to reach the code letter hidden in the misleads. One jump equals a letter, numeral, or other mark:

$$6 - M3>2REC - 5$$

When you see this < and the numeral which follows it, **go back** that number of jumps, but do not count the < as a jump:

$$4 + CA<168XP$$

With this code, EARTH might be clouded over like this:

$$6 - M3>2REC - 5$$
$$4 + CA<168XP$$
$$H>3BKR + 6$$
$$T<10 - 4$$
$$BHY<26 - D$$

Or even—egads!—like this:

$$6 - M3>2REC - 54 + CA<168XPH>3BKR + 6T<10 - 4BHY<26 - D$$

Try the Key: Crack the Codes

1
6>1S – 2
AM<2 + 3
3>23F
B>1E – X

2
LP3<3 + R
>2ME6
HQA5<2
= = V<1
4>3MGE

3
S5B3<4 + K
32>2PN – Y
07 + 5H<5
M>1R
K3<2000 +
EO – 3<4
O>5B + + DL

4
2>4R + 6J
UM308<5
30>24N
K + + 5<4 – LP
B>3PMI
OT5<2

5 S5+<3R>1H+5>3++ED=3<3–RX2D>1M>26AS++R<4>1K

6 >2MIN<1+B3>22T>1RU–P+6<5D<1+OE<15>2QR

MYSTERY MAPS

Muddle a meddler with a mystery map.

Print your message:

UNDER   THE   SAND   DUNES

Make up a place name for each letter or letter group in the message:

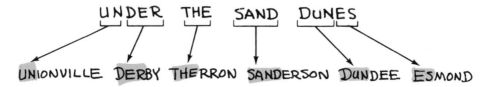

UNIONVILLE   DERBY   THERRON   SANDERSON   DUNDEE   ESMOND

Print the names in the order that a code-cracker should read them, from left to right, beginning at the top.

UNIONVILLE

DERBY   THERRON

SANDERSON

DUNDEE   ESMOND

Draw map lines, making sure a line goes through each place name at the point where the code letters are to be separated from the rest of the place name. If you wish, draw other map symbols as misleads.

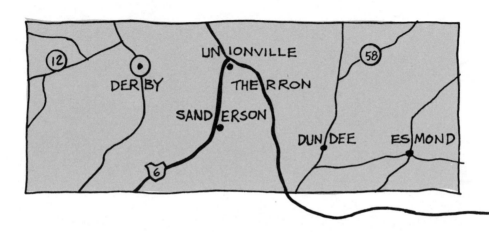

Try the Key: Crack the Codes

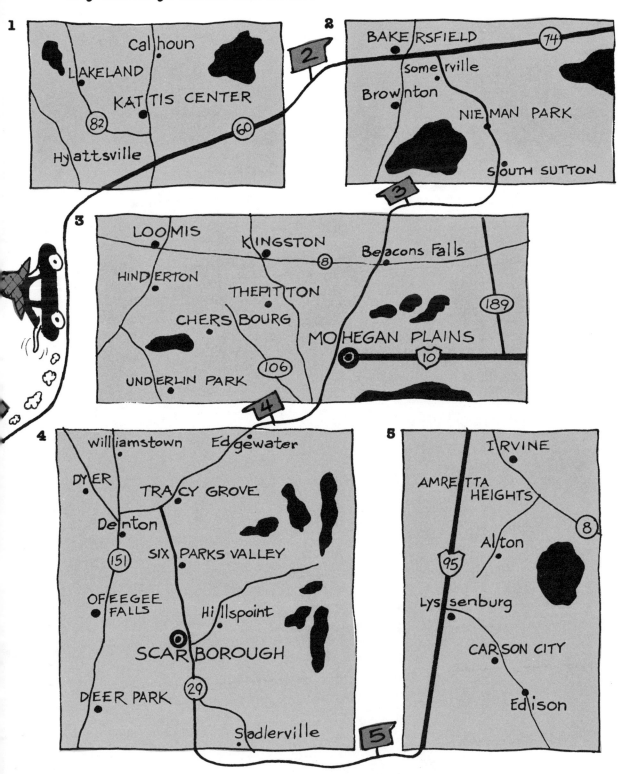

DERAILMENT!

A break. A switch. That's all there is to this code. But it's sure to topple snoops off the track.

Print the message you want to send. Number the letters like this:

```
1 2 3 1 2  3 1 2 3  1 2 3   1 2 3 1 2 3 1
H I T C H  Y O U R  N E W   C A B O O S E
```

Then rewrite the message, breaking the words into sets of three letters each, switching the second and third letter in each set:

```
1 2 3      1 3 2          1 2 3     1 3 2
H I T  →   H T I          C H Y  →  C Y H
```

If necessary, let the final letter or two stand alone or together. For example, the single E below is the last letter in CABOOSE.

```
1 3 2    1 3 2   1 3 2   1 3 2    1 3 2   1 3 2  1
H T I    C Y H   O R U   N W E    C B A   O S O  E
```

Try the Key: Crack the Codes

1 CPO YAC T
2 HTO PTO AOT
3 AYM LVO ETS IM
4 FRO GTE PSA SOW RD
5 WAH TTS HPE RCI E

6 DNO TIG VUE P
7 TEH SRU FSI LUO SY
8 POR MSI EEM YUO WLI L
9 WAH TJA EKR HIE S
10 IIL KYE OAU LTO

SWING RINGS

To read a message in this code, look at the clapper in each colored bell. It swings toward a  LETTER that's hidden in the code.
Bells left uncolored are misleads.

Try the Key: Crack the Code

What are long, wide-eyed looks to the sky?

YOU PUT THE STOPWATCH

BACK IN ROXANNE'S KNAPSACK

CROSS 'N TOSS 'EM

Here's how to cross up and puzzle a supersleuth.

1 Make a grid and place the letters of your message in the squares. Be sure of two things:

> The letters should read correctly from left to right, from top to bottom.
> A square should be left empty **before** each letter.

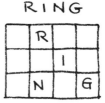

2 Color in the square that comes before each letter in the message. This is the signal that a Cracker Jack or Jill looks for.

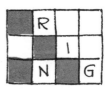

3 Toss in misleads that form as many other words or near-words as possible.

Try the Key: Crack the Code

Question: Why are those horses in the center ring?

Answer:

H	I		B		E	H		C		A	R	C
O		U		S		E	D		T		H	Y
M	A		E		Y	R		A		R	E	
E		T		H	O		E		M		A	S
R		N		E		E	V	A	L	U	E	
S	O		E		N	O	S	Y		T	E	R

CAN-SCANS

An electronic eye can't scan and crack this code, but your eyes can.

Look for each group of letters and numerals set off by double slash marks (/ /). In each group, note only **two** things, the <u>first</u> letter and the <u>first</u> numeral:

C—H35//

The letter C is part of a code word, and the numeral 3 shows the position of the letter in the word. The other letters and numerals in the group are misleads. Ignore them.

Here's how scanning works:

C—H35 // 5E-7-M // N-●1-BR // 2-67I // L-RB6-5 // 4-K-PM

C=3rd letter   E=5th   N=1st   I=2nd   L=6th   K=4th

N I C K E L
1 2 3 4 5 6

The ● stands for zero. It's colored in so that it can't be confused with the letter O. Pay no attention to it whenever it appears.

Try the Key: Crack the Codes

1.   D-4-56Y // 1-●MB // Y-65 // 3-●5-N // 2-OPX // 569-AZ

2.   YM-K-3 // 2-●4R // 1-6T-5   E-356 // 1-OPX-4 // N-2

3.   L-M65● // 2-AR // 7-66EQ // 346-D // T-1●●6 // 5-3O·X // PC-43X-N

4.   2-6LP // E-FF4 // B-T-16 // U-K3-4   N-X-3 // 1-●PY // E-KK2-6

KITTY-CORNERED

Here's a good code for all clever cats.

Break up your message by writing the letters in the opposite diagonal positions in a grid. Begin at the left square at the top.

D	N	F	E
T	E	I	E
R	G	T	H
D	E	T	O

To see how the letters are kitty-cornered, look at the numeral pattern in this grid——➤

1	3	5	7
9	11	13	15
16	14	12	10
8	6	4	2

Now follow this order in decoding the message.

1 = D
2 = O
3 = N
4 = T

As you go back and forth, you'll see that this message warns

DON'T FEED THE TIGER

Hint: If you are coding a message, count the number of letters and divide by 4. If you need to, add misleads at the end to make the division by 4 even. A message with 27 letters requires 1 mislead. The grid you draw will have 7 squares across and 4 down.

Try the Key: Crack the Codes

BEWARE! Some letters trailing at the end of a message may be sly little misleads.

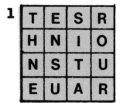

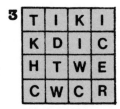
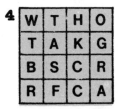

CLUB RULE#1

A	Y	I	W	O	N	E	S	H	S	L	B	U	T	T	L	T	M	S	E
P	E	R	T	H	W	R	S	H	C	P	S	F	O	O	E	O	N	T	E
R	H	O	A	T	N	M	R	S	A	H	I	W	D	O	E	T	E	C	S
E	K	E	I	L	A	A	S	M	U	C	I	T	R	T	E	H	D	K	N

KEY LINE PIES

Lined paper is perfect for these puzzlers. Write the alphabet letters in sets of three—ABC, DEF, and so on. On the first line below the alphabet draw round pies and number them in 1-2-3 order. On the second line, under the pies, write the number of the alphabet group, beginning with 1 for ABC.

ABC	DEF	GHI	JKL	MNO	PQR	STU	VWX	YZ%
①②③	①②③	①②③	①②③	①②③	①②③	①②③	①②③	①②③
1 1 1	2 2 2	3 3 3	4 4 4	5 5 5	6 6 6	7 7 7	8 8 8	9 9 9

Try the Key: Crack the Code

Dear Diary,

①③②   ①③③   ②②②   ③②③①   ③②②   ③   ③①②
1 6 2   9 5 7   7 3 2   5 5 4 9   5 5 2   3   1 1 5

①②①③②   ①①   ①②③③②①   ②③②②③   ③
7 3 1 6 2   5 9   7 2 1 6 2 7 7   8 3 7 3 9   3

②③②①②③③   ①③①②   ①②①②②③①①
8 5 5 2 2 6 9   4 7 7 7   9 2 7 7 2 6 2 1 9

①②③①   ①①③①   ③   ②①①   ②②③   ②②①②
8 2 6 1   7 1 3 2   3   8 1 7   3 2 6   1 2 7 7

③③③②①③   ②③②   ②③①①   ①②②   ①③②①
2 6 3 2 5 2 9   1 7 7   7 5 2 1 9   7 3 2   1 1 7 2 2

①①   ③③   ①②②   ①③①②②   ②②③②   ①②③
1 7   3 2   7 3 2   2 3 2 5 7   4 5 5 8   5 2 9

①③③②①   ③①
5 3 8 2 2   7 6

POLKA DOTS

Count the dots above and below each letter. If the sum is 3, then the letter is part of a SECRET MESSAGE.

Try the Key: Crack the Code

What makes a kid whirl and scratch?

SUE SPUN INTO THAT CRASH PAD!

SOME DRUMMERS!

As you parade words across a notebook page, let some of them march to a different beat. Just quickstep them this way:

1
Print or write each code word with the line passing through it:

~~like this~~

2
Build a misleading message around the code words. Make sure the misleads march straight along on the line.

In this example, the coded message is shown in color. See how each word in the message crosses the line.

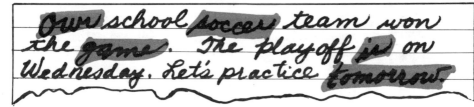

Our school soccer team won the game. The playoff is on Wednesday. Let's practice tomorrow.

Try the Key: Crack the Code

Dear Jim

Can you go to Frontier Park on Saturday? The old buildings there are fun to see. And the wooden bridge is just wide enough for a horse and buggy.

Can I count on you to take off at nine? Please be on your front steps. We'll pull up in the truck, and you can hop on board.

The truck will be a surprise. It is now a bright orange color. It's blinding!!!

Hope you'll be there... with your sunglasses on!

GRAPHODES

What are these lines jumping about? Do they show a pulse beat? An earthquake? A rickrack pattern? The size of shark teeth?

No, they're none of these. They're spy-zappers called graphodes.

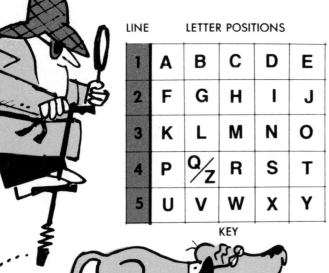

LINE	LETTER POSITIONS				
1	A	B	C	D	E
2	F	G	H	I	J
3	K	L	M	N	O
4	P	Q/Z	R	S	T
5	U	V	W	X	Y

KEY

The numeral in a graphode signal which key line to look across.

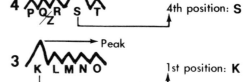

4 ⌇⌇⌇ ↳ Line 4   3 ⌇⌇ ↳ Line 3

The peak in a graphode signals the letter position in that key line.

4 P Q/Z R S T → Peak — 4th position: **S**

3 K L M N O → Peak — 1st position: **K**

Now that you know S and K are the first two letters, can you tell what's really jumping there?

Try the Key: Crack the Codes

1   4   2   3   5   3   1

2   3   3   4   2   1   2   4

3   2   4   1   1   4   2   3   1

4   1   5   4   4   3   2   2

5   1   2   3   1   4   1   3   1

ABRACADABACUS!

This key fits the abacus code, which works its magic much as a graphode does.

The numeral at the top of a bead column tells which key column to use. The biggest bead signals the letter position in the column.

For example:

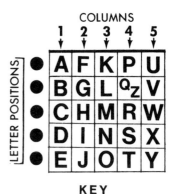

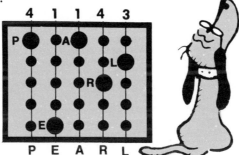

Try the Key: Crack the Codes

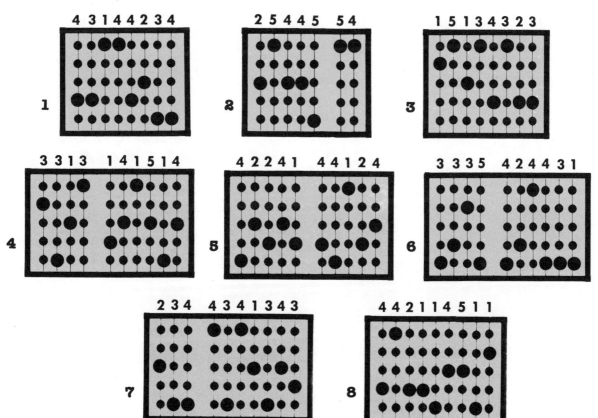

ON TARGET!

Target your message in a series of **sights**.

1 Write your message, and pair off the letters.

1 2 1   2 1 2 1 2 1
F I X   C A M E R A

2 Put each pair of letters, with their numerals,
in two sections, or quadrants, of a sight:

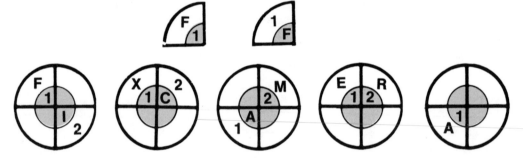

3 Add misleads by using the numerals 3 and 4 plus letters.
If a message does not end in a pair of letters, do not use
the numeral 2 in the last sight. Use 1, 3, 4, and 5.

Be sure to write the numeral one like this 1 or 1 or 1.

and the letter **I** like this I or I or *I*.

Try the Key: Crack the Codes

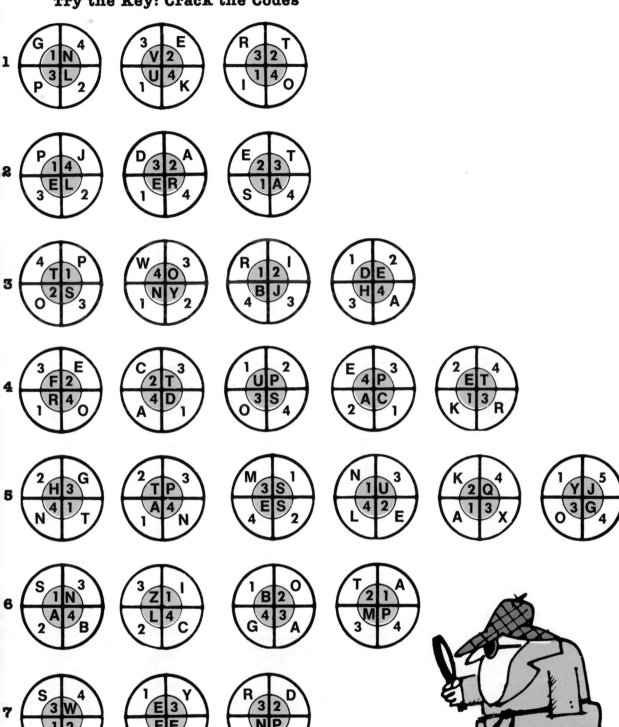

BUTTER-RIDDLE RIPPLE

Treat yourself to an ice cream code. It's butter-riddle ripple. And each ripple signals a code letter above it:

YUMMY

All other letters are misleads.

Try the Key: Crack the Codes

In each scoop, lick the ripples from top to bottom, left to right. Find the answer to the riddles.

28

DECODE-A-CLUE ISLANDS

How good a **cryptographer** (that's a big word for code-cracker)
have you become? Can you pass this test? Give it a try.

As you study the map, dig up clues that will drift the coded treasure
to the shores of your mind.

Hint: What you believe you see may not be the C in the sea you
see at all.

ANSWER FILE

CATER-RIDDLE-PILLAR, page 4
1 FURNACE
2 BUBBLE (three Bs, a -BLE, and U)
3 A WINK
4 SWARM ('s warm)

TOTEM POLES, page 5
1 DEAR CODE PAL READ EACH POLE
ON THIS PAGE
2 THEN YOU'LL LEARN THAT I'D LIKE
TO START A MAGAZINE
3 IT WILL BE WRITTEN ONLY IN CODES
THAT PAL CLUBBERS KNOW
4 WOULD YOU LIKE TO HELP WITH
THE FIRST ISSUE

BALLOON BUFFOON, pages 6-7
1 RING THE BELL
2 HAUNTED HOUSE
3 UNDER GOAL POSTS
4 STICK AROUND

SHOE BUSINESS? page 8
Example: IN DOUBLE-TALK

1 PACK A LUNCH
2 WAIT UNTIL DARK
3 RIDE THE FERRIS WHEEL
4 WHAT DID YOU GET
5 IT'S SO FUNNY
6 WHY SHOULD I
7 I HAVE PIERCED EARS
8 STICKBALL GAME AT SIX

Ghost Hunters, Inc.
CLUB MET ON MONDAY.
MEETING STARTED LATE.
EVERYONE BUT ROY
VOTED TO GO GHOST
HUNTING NEXT FRIDAY
NIGHT. MEETING ENDED AT
FIVE.